Pieces Of Me

Uncovering the Stories & Journeys We Hold Inside

Renu Chaudhary Shah

India | USA | UK

Made with ❤ on the BookLeaf Publishing Platform
www.bookleafpub.in
www.bookleafpub.com

Dedication

This is my first book—a piece of my soul, laid bare on these pages. And before anyone else, I dedicate it to the **Almighty God,** who has been my silent strength in the moments when I felt most alone, my guiding light when I couldn't see the way, and my quiet refuge when the world became too loud.

To the **Silent Warriors** who carry unseen battles yet refuse to give up.
To the dreamers who dare to question, to break free, to start again.
To the ones who live in the grey, navigating uncertainty, pain, and transformation.
To those who have ever felt unheard, unseen, or misplaced in their own lives—may you find yourself in these words, just as I found myself while writing them.

This book is more than poetry; it is a promise to myself and to you—that no matter how broken, lost, or uncertain we feel, every piece of us still matters.

May we all find peace in our own stories.

Preface

"Pieces of Me" is not just a collection of poems; it is a journey—a journey of self-discovery, reflection, and reclaiming the parts of myself I thought I had lost along the way. Every word here holds a piece of my past, my struggles, my growth, and the quiet strength I've found in the moments that seemed too small to matter.

Writing this book was never about seeking approval or validation from the outside world. It was about acknowledging the **pieces of myself** that I have often kept hidden, buried under layers of **societal expectations, family roles, and personal fears.** In this collection, I have chosen to speak my truth, even when it feels uncomfortable, and to embrace the grey areas of my life —the moments of **uncertainty, pain, and growth.**

These poems are a reflection of **my soul, my personal experiences, and my ongoing journey.** They are for anyone who has ever felt **lost, broken, or invisible.** For those who have wondered if there's more to life than the roles they've been cast into, and for those who, like me, have spent years searching for the strength to simply be.

Inside these pages, you will find poetry that speaks to the in-between moments of life—where we question, rediscover, and redefine ourselves. Poems like:

- Grey—Between the Lines
- God in Me
- Rarest of Rare
- Promise to Tiny Hands
- The Road
- Through the Lens of Paused Times
- The Forgotten Self—A Woman Reborn
- What Are We So Afraid Of?
- Unspoken Vows
- The Weight of Silence
- Unseen, Unshaken—Their Version Is Not Me
- Illusion of Perfection
- The Woman They Don't See
- The Four People
- Fear of Failing Before Even Starting
- In My Reflection Mode
- The Routine That Has No Name
- Priority
- Starting Again
- Cooking Disasters & Smoke Alarms
- Beyond Material

This book is an invitation to uncover the **stories and journeys we all carry inside**—stories that **shape us, heal us, and remind us that even in our darkest moments, we are not alone.**

Acknowledgements

I would like to express my deepest gratitude to those who have supported me throughout this journey.

To my family, who has always been my anchor—my **Mother and Father,** whose love, wisdom, and sacrifices have shaped me into the person I am today. Your unwavering belief in me has been my guiding light. To my **Brothers,** who have stood by me in ways both seen and unseen, your strength and support mean more than words can express.

To my **Husband,** without whom this book would not have come into existence. Your presence, in ways both profound and subtle, has played an undeniable role in this journey.

To my **children, Rudra & Mahi,** whose laughter and innocence remind me daily of the beauty of life and the importance of staying true to myself. You are my greatest inspiration.

To the Friends who have listened, encouraged, and held space for my fears and dreams—thank you for reminding me that vulnerability is not a weakness but a strength.

And to every person who has crossed my path, whether in joy or in sorrow, you have all shaped the woman I am today.

Finally, to myself, for not giving up, for embracing the grey, and for trusting that the pieces of me, however broken or incomplete, are enough. This book is a testament to the healing power of storytelling, and I hope it serves as a reminder that we all have the power to rewrite our narratives, **One piece at a time.**

1. Grey - Between the Lines

In the world between black and white,
Lies a shade, soft yet *infinite.*
Not darkness, nor light,
But the *whispers* of day meeting night.

Grey is the pause, the in-between,
Where *truth* and *illusion* convene.
The color of thoughts untold,
Of *silent battles,* quiet but bold.

There was a time I fought the waves,
Resisted storms, refused to bend.
But *life wears you down,*
Till you nod, smile, and just pretend.

I agreed when they said the *sky was red,*
Though I knew it had always been blue.
But when I dared to see it different,
I *swallowed my voice, like I always do.*

Not because I didn't feel,
But because feeling became too much.
So I let the world move as it pleased,
While I stood still, *untouched.*

Yes, **I am Grey and proud to be,**
A soul that walks in harmony.
Balancing worlds, *step by step,*
Living my truth with *what is kept.*

They pull, they push, they try to mend,
Forgetting—**I am not theirs to bend.**
Yet in their smiles, I find my way,
And that makes the journey stay.

Grey is not escape nor surrender,
It is the space *where I learn.*
Not lost, not whole, but still standing,
Even when I go *unseen.*

For in **Grey, we learn to see,**
The depth of life's uncertainty.
Neither lost nor wholly found,
In Grey, we find the middle ground.

Grey is the silence I've become,
Grey is the color of being numb.

2. God in Me

Unseen, unknown, it softly flies,
Or assembles in faith where perception lies.
How real it is, who knows, who saw?
A silent force, beyond earthly law.

The stories told, the lessons shared,
Through whispers of faith, I was prepared.
I lived, I believed, in someone, somewhere,
A presence unseen, yet always there.

But then, *why hurt? Why tears unshed?*
Is it no one, nowhere, where my prayers are led?
Or is it a waiting, a time to align,
A period of change, both yours and mine?

My belief system, a world so unique,
Perception and experience shape what I seek.
Sometimes I connect, *feel divinely whole,*
Yet bad experiences weigh on my soul.

Thinking *empathy*, time after time,
But not all hearts echo mine.
I'm available, like God, for all who call,
Yet the **God in me** breaks, *I too can fall.*

Through trials faced, I begin to see,
Experience shapes the **God in me.**
And when the storms turn calm and still,
I feel it's divine, *a guiding will.*

But what am I to do with all I own?
How much is mine, how much is known?
How much is enough, how much remains?
Am I *rich in things—or rich in chains?*

The books we read, the knowledge gained,
The lands we cross, the worlds explained—
Yet, have we explored the depths within?
Or do we exploit the soul we've been?

Does being a saint mean I must depart—
To forests deep, where rivers start?
To temples high, or mountains steep,
To find the peace I long to keep?

No, *I believe the path is near,*
Not in escape, but facing fear.

For **running away is not the key—**
But embracing flaws with honesty.

No masks to wear, no roles to play,
No need to mend, no need to stay.
For **God's not far, nor lost at sea—**
He whispers soft—He lives in me.

The **saint in me** serves, gives and stays,
Fulfilling debts in endless ways.
A silent vow, a duty spun,
To care for all—till all is done.

And when the weight is set aside,
I dream to roam, to run, to hide.
But what is life beyond these chains?
Is it *gold, or wealth, or fleeting gains?*

Perhaps it's not answers, but lessons *profound,*
In the flow of life, where **faith is found.**
For even in doubt, there's space to believe,
That **God in me helps me perceive.**

One life bestowed, a *gift* to keep,
Not just in duty, not just in sleep.
So **why not live—not just survive?**
Why wait till later—to feel alive?

For still, **I rise from pain and despair,**
For the **God in me is always there.**

3. Rarest of Rare

It's a powerful phrase, often said,
When the law decides who's guilty, who's dead.
But who decides what's truly rare?
The victim? The judge? Or those who were there?

Every story in the news I read
Makes me wonder whose pain runs deepest indeed.
Is it the one who lost their life?
Or those left behind to carry the strife?

What about the one who caused it all—
What pain pushed them to take that fall?
What broke so badly inside their mind,
That they chose to leave all kindness behind?

When it's someone close, *it cuts so deep,*
The pain stays awake, never letting you sleep.
It feels so rare, so heavy to bear,
Like no one else could ever compare.

But when it's someone else, far away,
It's easier to judge what led them astray.
We don't see their tears, their hidden fight,
We just see headlines, decide what's right.

So many lives with **stories untold,**
So many truths *waiting to unfold.*
I read and wonder, *"Am I better off,*
Because I'm not the one carrying this cross?"

Yet, I have my own story, my own pain,
With losses, struggles, and lessons to gain.
We all have scars, some deep, some bare,
In life's great web, *we're all somewhere rare.*

The **rarest of rare** isn't just law's decree,
It's *the pain we carry, the things we don't see.*
Behind every face is a battle, a tear,
And that's what makes each life so rare.

4. Promise to Tiny Hands

Everyone is working and so am I,
But when the tooth is lost, and the questions fly,
It's the mother who weaves the tale,
Of **tooth fairies and struggles,** without fail.

From classes to classes, I'm running with time,
Carrying it all, *be it sunshine or grime.*
Food, clothes, snacks and blankets too,
Comfort and care in everything I do.

No boundaries of time, whenever I rise,
Work begins under endless skies.
Even the car becomes my little space,
Where exhaustion fades, *a fleeting embrace.*

Watching my kids from a distance there,
As they run toward me, beyond compare.
Everything pauses—it's their time now,
My miseries and commitments take a bow.

I can't thank God enough for my kids,
They're my light, *my reason to live.*
Whatever I'm given, I'd put on the stake,
To ensure *they're not a mistake I make.*

My new identity is **mother,** and how it's true,
It made me kind, *a better version, renewed.*
From animals to humans, from ancient to now,
Motherhood transforms, teaching the *"how."*

With every effort, with all my might,
I guide them forward, I hold them tight.
From my experience, I do my best,
To give them *more* and handle the rest.

Life to this life, that's what I give,
Through every moment, *I teach how to live.*
Even when sadness weighs me down,
I hide it with a smile, *never let them frown.*

Even when my back aches or my heart feels sore,
Or my mind's in turmoil, battling one thing more,
I push through the pain, no chance to *rewind,*
For the title of **mother,** I leave nothing behind.

The physical changes, the hormonal strain,
The battles I fight, *again and again.*

And then comes the shame, the world points out,
How far is it fair to twist and shout?

But still, I stand, **filling the gaps,**
For every moment they need, I map.
No looking back, there's more to fight,
For my *promotion as mom,* I'll hold tight.

Promise to Tiny Hands—it's more than a name,
It's love, it's strength, *it's playing the game.*
It's running ahead while carrying all,
And standing tall, *no matter how small.*

Trying is not always *achieving,*
And falling is *not always failing.*
Little I know, but I give more,
While keeping my energy intact, *even in the roar.*

So I fill their lives with **laughter and cheer,**
With every step, *I face my fear.*
For the tiny hands that *grasp* my own,
I give my heart, my strength, *all I've known.*

Promise to Tiny Hands—a vow so true,
To give them life in all that I do.
Through every trial, through every fight,
I promise to guide them *to the light.*

5. The Road

As I sit in the car, I watch it all fly by,
Polls, trees and road concrete, under the sky.
It's peaceful, almost like time's on pause,
My mind starts to wander, without a cause.

Thoughts unclear, like a blurry view,
But a ray of light breaks through.
Like cars on the road, passing by fast,
I move forward, not looking back at the past.

Unlearning's harder than learning something new,
Letting go of old thoughts, it's tough to do.
Vivid memories pile up, they stay,
While the real work seems to fade away.

I try to guide others and myself too,
But clarity's lost, as I search for the view.
Reality's shaped by others' eyes,
Their approval and thoughts cloud my skies.

On the road, I see flowers and trails,
Bound by the roads, where life prevails.
Dividers to stop, but I want to know,
What lies ahead, where will I go?

Everyone's running, chasing their dreams,
But their faces look empty, or so it seems.
Is it their life, or just my perception,
A reflection of the world in its own direction?

The horns, the noise, all around me,
Where's it coming from, what's it supposed to be?
In the crowd, there are signals and lights,
So many colors flashing, so many fights.

Some build, some destroy, to make something new,
Taking someone's dreams or building their view.
But still, we move, trying to find our way,
In this world of construction, where hopes decay.

The road keeps moving, with all its sound,
Signals and signs, in chaos unbound.
I wonder what's real, what's just noise,
But I keep going, searching for my voice.

In the crowd, I'm not alone,
We all have stories, we all have grown.

The road's not just ahead, it's inside me too,
And maybe, just maybe, it's the same for you.

14

6. Through the Lens of Paused Times

I cry at movies, at stories unknown,
Yet in my own world, I stand alone.
How strange it is—to feel so deep,
Yet with the ones I know, *silence* keeps.

How life shifts in a single breath,
How we hand over power till there's nothing left.
Why do we give someone the right to define,
To bend our will, to steal our shine?

I still remember childhood days,
The laughter, the light, the simple ways.
A time untouched, so raw, so true,
Before the world taught me what I never knew.

Simple things, simple thoughts—
We took words as they were taught.
Now we're expected to read between,
Left misunderstood, unheard, unseen.

People hide behind their pride,
Afraid to speak, to clarify.
They choose confusion, call it grace,
Modernity with an **empty face.**

Those school days—those pencils with erasers,
Pencils like us, carving our traces.
And erasers—our parents' hands so tight,
Guiding, correcting, making things right.

How badly I wish to relive that phase,
To step back into those golden days.
But why is it that one part of life
Becomes the one we yearn to revive?

On the other side, it's better they stay,
The past, a memory, bright as day.
For some things can never return,
And living there makes the **future burn.**

Sometimes, when we reach for that time,
The magic is gone, no longer sublime.
What once felt true, what once felt near,
Now fades into shadows, clouded by fear.

We are all the sum of what's been done,

A journey of scars, both lost and won.
Past experiences shape who we are,
Good or bad, they've left their mark,
Though we may bend, we grow and learn,
From bad memories, we start to discern.

But even so, we find ourselves trapped,
In patterns of pain, in cycles perhaps.
Trusting life, trusting the heart,
We give chances, and then fall apart.
For some lessons, it seems we must repeat,
Until the consequences feel complete.

The circle of life keeps turning still,
Memories float, but they don't fulfill.
The present is the only lens that's true,
To move, to heal, to start anew.
For what has passed is not our chain,
It's only wisdom dressed in pain.

Was it the fancies of a world so bright,
Or the peace within that felt so right?
The heart so pure, the soul so free,
Before the weight of reality.

When we did not have to prove, we were free,
But why must we prove now, and for what should it be?

Who set the rules, who made the game?
Why must we chase **validation's name?**

We grow up thinking all is well,
That what we are is where we'll dwell.
And then one day, the truth arrives—
The world outside was built on lies.

We change, we bend, we learn to hide,
The innocence lost, the truth denied.
But who is to blame for this shift so wide?
The world? The pain? Or the trust inside?

I have changed—a lot—my face, my mind,
The mirror speaks of passing time.
Yet deep inside, I am still that child,
Running free, unchained, wild.

In the farm, I wait my turn,
To slide on sand, to feel the burn,
To run with open hands so wide,
To chase the wind, to touch the sky.

I am still connected, I know my place,
I've found my roots, I've found my peace.
Though the world may shift, and I may bend,
I'll never break—I'll rise again.

7. The Forgotten Self - A Woman Reborn

I was never weak—just made to believe so,
Told to shrink, to smile, to go with the flow.
They wrote my limits in ink, bold and fine,
But forgot—this story is mine.

I thanked those who walked away,
For they cleared the path to my own way.
No more waiting, no more doubt,
I've found my fire—I'm burning out loud.

One-man army? Hell, I own the fight,
With battle scars that shine in light.
I don't need saving, don't need a guide,
I hold the compass, I decide.

I will dream enough to shake the ground,
Break the chains, tear walls down.
No need for permission, no need for grace,
I carve my world, I take my space.

Fear? It'll sit and watch me rise,
Struggle? It'll fuel these fearless eyes.
Rejection? Oh, let it come,
I've danced with doubt, now watch me run.

It's never too late to start or restart,
To rewrite the rules, to own my part.
They may not hear, but they will see,
A woman unleashed—wild and free.

I pick my pieces, I build, I claim,
No one erases my strength, my name.
Storms may come, but I will sail,
Not just survive—I will prevail.

My wings are open, the sky is wide,
I am my own—I stand with pride.

8. What Are We So Afraid Of?

We talk about justice.
We talk about education.
We talk about a world where wrong is wrong.

But when the moment comes—we freeze.

We see, we hear, we KNOW.
Yet, we turn away.
Why?

Because stepping in might mean losing a friend,
Breaking a family,
Taking a side we don't want to admit exists.
Because speaking up comes with a cost,
And silence is the easier currency.

Since when did helping become a crime?
Since when did choosing truth become dangerous?
Which education taught us to stay silent?

Which culture taught us to abandon those in need?

We let people suffer in silence,
Afraid that if we help—we will lose something.
But tell me, what kind of humanity is this,
Where we weigh our relationships
Against someone's pain
And choose to walk away?

What are we so afraid of?

Losing people who protect the guilty?
Losing the comfort of ignorance?
Losing the illusion that this does not happen in our
homes,
To our people, by our people?

Enough.
No more looking away.
No more choosing silence over truth.
No more letting fear be stronger than what is right.

Because the real loss is not a relationship.
The real loss is our own humanity.

And I refuse to lose mine.

Yet, when someone wants to help, they are called too
available.
When no one stands up, they are called wise for staying
out of it.

What kind of world is this,
Where kindness is weakness,
And silence is strength?

But listen—
I am not here to be wise.
I am not here to stay silent.
I am here to stand for you.

I will not turn my back.
I will not pretend I did not see.
I will not let fear decide if I should help.

I will be your voice when yours shakes.
I will be your strength when you are drained.
I will stand by you—
In need and indeed.

Call me.
Count on me.
Not because I have nothing else to do,
But because I know what I say—

And I know what it means.

Because I refuse to be another pair of closed eyes,
Another silent witness,
Another person who looks away.

I choose to stand.
I choose to speak.
I choose to be the difference—
Because someone must.

And if standing with you costs me people,
Then so be it.
Because silence is the only side
I will never stand on.

9. Unspoken Vows

You think you know what love is?
A bond that's pure, they say.
A promise made in sacred vows,
But let me tell you, it's all play.

I see the lies behind those smiles,
The mask you wear—cracked and frail.
You speak of trust, of hearts that bind,
But inside, it's a war, a tale of betrayal.

I carry your weight, your unspoken sin,
Your secrets you think I can't see within.
But know this now—***I'm no fool,***
I don't bend, I don't follow your rules.

You talk about loyalty, respect,
But I've learned to stand without regret.
I don't need your validation, your praise,
I carve my own path, in my own ways.

I do not need your approval, not on my character,
Nor society's, for I have my own mirror.
My work speaks for me, my duties align,
I stand on my own—my life, my design.

You break me with words, with silence deep,
But I'm no shadow, no victim to keep.
I feel the rage—oh, how it burns,
But I'm not the one who'll crash and churn.

You see, I'm too proud to stoop that low,
To meet you in your twisted show.
I keep my dignity, I keep my peace,
While your world crumbles, I won't cease.

I lived too long in your judgment's grip,
Taught to fear what others think,
But no more—I've shed that skin,
No longer your pawn, your broken thing.

I rise. I stand. I take the lead,
I don't beg, I don't plead.
You can try to break, to bend, to tear,
But you'll find me standing—unaware.

So keep your chains, your lies, your games,
I'm done with playing in your name.

The bond you spoke of, it's gone to dust,
I know my worth, and it's built on trust.

So when you ask what love can be,
Know this—love doesn't silence me.
It's power, it's strength, it's standing tall,
And I'll rise higher—**above it all.**

10. The Weight of Silence

They come first, I come last,
Like a shadow fading fast.
Was I ever enough to be seen,
Or just a name lost in between?

If only they had believed in me,
Seen my worth beyond what they see.
Maybe then, I could have flown,
Not just watched, standing alone.

Why must I explain what I do,
As if my worth is theirs to review?
Whatever they give, it weighs me down,
A silent favor, a heavy crown.

In my world, I am just a passing thought,
Out in the crowd, still left to rot.
Mistakes are made by all, yet see—
The mirror only reflects mine to me.

When someone, somewhere, doesn't like me,
The crowd joins in so easily.
Instead of lifting, they push me deep,
Turning their backs while I silently weep.

When I stood by them in their pain,
It came with a price I can't explain.
Now they feel they own my voice,
As if my silence was ever my choice.

If sorrow fills me, how do I fake,
A smile that's not mine to make?
Yet I do—because I must,
Burying my grief in layers of dust.

A lifetime spent in waiting halls,
Seeking nods, breaking walls.
Even for what was mine, I fought,
Struggling alone for what I sought.

Where do I stand, in love or in chains?
Where is the bond, and where are the stains?
A place should hold, not tear apart,
Yet here I stand—with a silent heart.

11. Unseen, Unshaken— Their Version Is Not Me

Born into love, yet never my own,
A daughter first, in a house not home.
Taught to give, to bend, to stay,
To shrink myself and obey.
Then comes marriage—a shift, a fall,
A new house, new rules—I adjust to all.
Changed my name, my voice, my tone,
Yet my own home? Never my own.

And then, a child—a love so deep,
Nights of sacrifice, no time for sleep.
They say, "You must know, it's a mother's role."
But when did parent become just **mother** alone?
I never went to classes, no lessons were taught,
Yet love made me learn what could never be bought.
Not just by birth, but by effort and care,
Yet how much we give—depends on what's there.

The days are long, the questions don't end,

A constant referee, a fixer, a friend.
Quarrels to settle, lessons to teach,
From math to morals, I cover each.
Doctor, chef, storyteller, guide—
No break, no pause, just shifting tides.

They whisper, "She's let herself go,"
As if my body was theirs to own.
They don't see the weight I bear—
Not just in pounds, but in love and care.
Stretch marks, fatigue, a slower pace,
Yet still, I run in life's endless race.
Hormones shift, yet I stand tall,
Because quitting? That's not me at all.

I don't "earn," so they say I lack,
Yet I build futures without looking back.
If I step out, they call it tight,
If I stay in, I "don't know life."
Schedules twist, stretch, and break,
Yet I rise again, for my children's sake.
No help, no pause, no guiding hand,
Yet I move forward—I **command.**

Their version of me is not me.
They see my silence, call it weak,
Not the storms I dare not speak.

They paint a picture, frame it tight,
A version of me in black and white.
A woman who bends, who takes it all,
Yet I refuse to be this small.
I am fire, I am free,
Their version of me is not me.

So don't question my strength, don't doubt my grind,
I carry the weight with power defined.
No cheers, no praise, no standing ovation,
Yet I **lead** this world—**my own creation**.

12. Illusion of Perfection

They weighed me down with their words,
Judged my worth before I spoke.
"Too strong, too soft, too much, too less,"
A game they play—just to impress.

A girl must bow but stand up tall,
A woman must give yet have it all.
They build a cage, call it grace,
Then judge the fire on my face.

If I work or not, how is it yours?
You don't run my home, you don't fight my wars.
People need to grow, open their eyes—
Even those in golden frames have cracks inside.

Everyone's a celebrity in their own way,
Yet they act like they hold the say.
If I don't wear a brand, so what?
If you do, does it make you a God?

We don't eat brands, we don't eat gold,
Peace is the prize, the realest goal.
What you own won't write your name,
If respect is lost in shallow games.

They call it perfection, but it's just a lie,
A mask they wear, afraid to try.
Point fingers at me, but if I turn,
Your glass castles will crash and burn.

They chase illusions, polished and bright,
Dressing up shadows to shine in the light.
But perfection fades, and truth remains,
And I refuse to play their games.

So no need to be perfect—flaunt your flaws,
No one can make you, no one can break your cause.
I choose not to owe anyone illusion,
I am me—without permission, without confusion.

13. The Woman They Don't See

They see the **smile**, not the sigh,
The grace, not the battles I fight inside.
They hear my voice in soft replies,
Never the **storms** I push aside.

They count the meals, the clothes I fold,
Not the **dreams** I had to hold.
They praise the child, the house so neat,
Yet never ask if **I've had a seat**.

They call me **strong**, yet take for free
The strength that slowly unbuilds me.
They say, *"She's fine, she never breaks,"*
Yet don't see the **toll** that silence takes.

I have been **something to everyone,**
A daughter, a friend, a mother, a guide.
A pillar to lean on, a shadow to hide in,
A voice of comfort, a hand by their side.

But when I look within, **I see a void,**
A silence where I should have been.
In giving them pieces, I lost my **whole**,
In making them smile, I buried **my dream.**

They see the **mother,** never the girl,
The one who once dreamed of **ruling the world.**
They see the hands that soothe, that serve,
Not the hands that once had **nerve.**

They say, *"She's lucky, she has it all,"*
Yet don't see the **weight beneath the walls.**
They see the patience, never the cost,
They see the love, but not what's **lost.**

I **did not do good** to myself—
And world, **this is not done.**
I carried your weight, I bore your storms,
But where was I when **I came undone?**

Not once did I ask, *What do I need?*
Not once did I stop to **simply breathe.**
They called me strong, they called me kind,
Yet no one asked — *was I ever mine?*

So now, **I stand,** I turn, I see,

A stranger staring back at me.
And I whisper softly, *it's time to be...*
Not just for them, but finally — **me.**

I am here, beneath it all,
Not just for others — **I stand tall.**
Not just a shadow, soft and small,
I am **the woman they don't see at all.**

14. The Four People

Throughout my life, I've searched in vain,
For four voices that whisper my name.
They speak in shadows, they judge, they claim,
Yet I've never seen a single face.

Whatever I wear, or talk, or eat,
I was made to think of those four before me.
My personality, my attitude—no longer mine,
Shaped by their words, confined by their lines.

From head to toe, from rise to set,
Life and routine became their silhouette.
Each step measured, each thought restrained,
Living for their nods, bound by their chains.

But let's say I lived as per them,
Bent my will to be their gem.
Lost myself in the process deep,
So they would like me—but did they?

They shape my choices, they weigh me down,
They write my story without a sound.
But when I cried, when I fell apart,
Not one of them was near my heart.

Where are they? Let us meet—
Will I change, or will you be?
Let's stand face to face, no masks, no lies,
So I no longer fear unseen eyes.

You held my dreams, you caged my flight,
You made me doubt my own right.
But today I rise, today I see—
The four of you were never real, only fear in me.

So now I walk, unchained, unbound,
No voices hold me, no whispers loud.
For those who mattered, they stood, they stayed—
And those four shadows just fade away.

15. Fear of Failing Before Even Starting

They tell you to wait, to be sure, to be wise,
To measure each step, to silence your rise.
They warn of the fall before you even take flight,
Casting their doubts, dimming your light.

The fear of failing before even starting
Chains the bold, stops the daring.
Not the fall, but the fear of the fall,
Not the loss, but never trying at all.

What if you stumble? What if you break?
What if your dream is a costly mistake?
But what if you soar? What if you shine?
What if the world was waiting for your time?

They say success is for the chosen few,
But the truth is—it's for those who push through.
The artist who paints, the leader who dares,
The mother who builds, the dreamer who cares.

No age is less, no age is more,
The present is time—nothing before.
The soldier who marches, the student who learns,
The fearless who fight for the life they yearn.

So step, stumble, rise, repeat—
The world is yours, not just a seat.
No more waiting, no more halting,
No more fear of failing before even starting.

Because failure is not in the loss or the pain,
But in never daring to play the game.

16. In My Reflection Mode

I sit in silence, a pause so rare,
No noise, no rush—just me and the air.
The world still moves, fast and unkind,
But here I stand, searching my mind.

The mirror shows a face I know,
Yet somewhere lost, yet somewhere grown.
Is this the me I meant to be?
Or just a shadow they made of me?

I trace the scars, the lessons learned,
The bridges built, the ones that burned.
Every tear, every fall,
Carved the story I now recall.

I gave, I loved, I stood so tall,
Yet sometimes felt like nothing at all.
Was I enough? Did I belong?
Or did I just play brave for too long?

I need time, not to rush, not to run,
Not to chase a race already won.
Not to meet expectations blind,
But to sit, to breathe, to find my mind.

The world is fast, the moments slip,
We hold, we lose, we let them dip.
Love feels rushed, words feel light,
Connections fade into the night.

I need time—not to explain,
Not to justify, not to feign.
Just to exist, just to be,
To know myself, to set me free.

So let me pause, let me stay,
In my own time, in my own way.
No past, no weight, no debts to pay,
Just me, in my reflection today.

17. The Routine That Has No Name

I wake up each morning, fresh and bright—
Oh wait, that's a lie, let's get it right.
I wake up because I have to, not by choice,
Two alarms I ignore and kids' loud noise.

"Mom, where's my socks?" "Mom, my tie!"
"Mom, my project!" Oh God, let me die.
Breakfast burns, the clock runs fast,
I drop them to school—**freedom at last!**

But wait, what freedom? The chores begin,
The cleaning, the folding, the laundry spin.
Dishes that multiply, floors that betray,
Didn't I mop this just yesterday?

I try to walk, a self-care dream,
Until the phone rings—"Maa, my ice cream?"
Then back home, to the work unseen,
Adjust, arrange—like I was never just eighteen.

By three, my me-time takes a final breath,
I pick them up, prepare for their tests.
"Mom, I'm hungry!" "Mom, my shoe's lost!"
"Mom, I spilled paint!" Lord, what's the cost?

Evening hits, my tea goes cold,
Dinner's a debate—Eat or be sold!
Bedtime is near, but not quite in sight,
One wants water, one needs light.

And in between, I teach, I scold, I pray,
Manners, behavior—shaping their way.
The world expects it all from a mother alone,
As if she must build a home on her own.

The work I do has no real name,
No title, no pay cheque, yet still the same.
If someone asks, "What did you do today?"
I smile, for what is there to say?

But if I'm away, and they step in my place,
Suddenly, there's a list—a long, panicked race!
Each task counted, each effort displayed,
Oh, now they see the work unpaid.

Kids are growing fast, and so am I,

Juggling it all, with a deep exhale and a sigh.
Finally, silence—I sit and stare,
Scrolling my phone, lost in mid-air.

Tomorrow's waiting, just the same,
A cycle, a loop, with no real name.
But in this madness, this unplanned flow,
Lies the love I'll miss when they grow.

So I sigh, I smile, I take what I get,
Because this messy, crazy life—it's the best one yet.

18. Priority

Once, my world was small—
painted with colors of toys and dreams,
where laughter echoed louder than time,
and **every wish felt within reach.**

Then life whispered change,
and my hands filled with tasks,
chasing goals, chasing moments,
chasing a future I thought I wanted.

Yes and no—two simple words,
yet shaped by shifting tides.
I learned that **saying yes to one dream
meant saying no to another.**

And all our lives, we are given choices—
loud ones that demand instant answers,
quiet ones that creep in unnoticed.
Every yes, every no,
every step we take

shapes not just what happens to us,
but **who we become.**

Yet, some choose to turn away,
pretending they don't see
the responsibilities waiting for them.
They move through life **untouched,**
drifting, distracting, delaying—
not because they cannot give,
but *because they do not want to.*

But time, a patient teacher,
showed me what remains—
when the rain falls hard,
when the world looks away,
when success feels silent—
family still stands, **unshaken.**

They are *the roots, the steady ground,*
the warmth that never fades.
Yet, how often do we forget,
letting life pull us away,
trusting they will always wait?

Freedom is not an escape from duty,
not a license to forget what must be done.
True freedom comes with understanding—

that happiness isn't just about the self,
but **about those who walk beside us,**
who wait for us,
who need us, even in silence.

We may think all is well,
that life moves forward regardless.
But **fulfillment isn't found in avoidance—**
it's found in **presence,**
in showing up,
in choosing to be there before it's too late.

Priorities are not just lists,
they are *maps of the heart.*
And if we listen, truly listen,
they will *lead us home—*
where we were meant to belong all along.

Because **the time we ignore today**
is **the time we'll never get back tomorrow.**

19. Starting Again

By now, life is clearer, *mapped in lines,*
Married or not, no more confines.
The kids have grown, they need you less,
Yet, somehow, **life still feels a mess.**

A decade lost to home and care,
Now, stepping out—**do I dare?**
Friends have soared, *they've built their name,*
While **I must start from dust again.**

Once, I worked *without a thought,*
No fear, no weight, no second shot.
Now, age whispers, **"Not so fast,"**
Bound by ties, by shadows cast.

A *job search maze* with no clear way,
New sites, new rules—*a fresh dismay.*
Options scattered, *none in sight,*
Just endless scrolling, left to right.

And if I dare to *carve a space*,
Home pulls back with *soft embrace*.
"You were here, you've always been,
Why change now? Stay unseen."

Yet something stirs, *a silent call,*
A *need to rise, to stand up tall.*
Not just *mother, not just wife,*
But once again—**my own life.**

20. Cooking Disasters & Smoke Alarms

They said, **"Shaadi ke baad sab seekh jaogi,"**
But nobody gave me a manual—*why? Oh why?*
Thrown into a kitchen with **spices unknown,**
Standing there **clueless, completely on my own.**

Back then, **studies were my only race,**
Degrees in hand, *full of grace.*
Math, science, history—**I mastered them all,**
Yet in the kitchen, **I hit a wall!**

Garam masala, jeera—what do they do?
Even Google said, *"Madam, I can't help you!"*
Scrolling recipes, **lost in translation,**
Yet my dish still ends in **devastation.**

Back home, *rotis were fluffy and fat,*
But here, *they're paper-thin—imagine that!*
"Yeh kya banaya?" they laugh and scoff,
"Is this a chapati or a hockey puck knockoff?"

One day, *daal should be thick and bold,*
Next day, *"Why so much tadka? It's too cold!"*
Even sabzi **plays a confusing game,**
Yesterday's favorite, today's shame!

And then they say, "Didn't you learn at home?"
Yes, because *my parents had psychic syndrome?*
How would they teach me *food from this land,*
When even *they never held it in their hand?!*

No mother-in-law, *no sisters, no guiding light,*
Just expectations that I'd get it right!
A *treasure hunt with no map in sight,*
Yet they wonder why my rotis give them a fright!

A decade later, **even today,**
If asked to judge that cuisine, *I sway.*
All my degrees, yet here I stand,
No training for this—wasn't that grand?!

Every bite feels like a **MasterChef test,**
And I'm still waiting to *"impress the guest!"*
Smoke alarms still cheer me on,
My kitchen battles are never gone.

Trial and error, mostly error, I fear,
But hey, *Swiggy and Zomato are always near!*
54

21. Beyond Material

The road stretches wide, my hands on the wheel,
The hum of the engine, the freedom I feel.
Music to my soul, a melody so sweet,
The rhythm of life, where joy and heart meet.

The taste of good food, the spice in the air,
The touch of the earth, without a care.
In the village, where the sand kisses rain,
The smoke from a fire, a memory's chain.

Desert trails whisper, calling me near,
A bath from the tubewell, water crystal clear.
The earthy fragrance, the land's soft embrace,
The waterfall's song, nature's own grace.

With my near ones my heart beats strong,
In the hammock, I read, where time moves along.
Sipping moments under stars, with music so light,
The world fades away in that peaceful night.

What's the point of grand houses, with walls that speak
loud,
Big cars that promise speed, yet leave us lost in the
crowd?
Balances that never balance, numbers that strain,
Chasing after dreams that only bring pain.

The world spins with glitter, with things we collect,
But in the end, what does it all reflect?
We hoard and we chase, as time slips away,
Yet the earth calls us softly to return one day.

Everything around us, full of material chase,
But nothing we hold can define our true place.
For in the end, we return to the land,
To merge with the earth, and let go of command.

So what's the point in all we possess?
When peace is found in simplicity's caress.
We've lost the essence, the nature of grace,
It's not in what we own, but in where we embrace.

The world keeps moving, but I'll choose to be still,
In nature's arms, finding peace, finding will.
The hustle may call, but I hear the soft plea—
To return to the earth, where I can simply be.

What we own, what we claim, will stay behind,

But peace is found in the quiet, the open mind.

In the earth, in the water, in the breeze that blows,

I find the essence of life, where true happiness grows.

www.ingramcontent.com/pod-product-compliance
Lightning Source LLC
LaVergne TN
LVHW041231200726
843507LV00013B/2649